104 Days of the Pandemic

Poems from March 19th through June 30th, 2020.

Daniel Damiano

"This collection provides us a wonderful opportunity to reflect on the emotions of the pandemic through an assortment of delicate and ferocious moments captured daily since March."
- *Creative Drive Podcast*

"Lovely and very powerful. It speaks of a collective experience and truth that, though Damiano makes very personal, can be a reflection for us all in our individual experiences. - Reading his words is in many ways healing and cathartic, a way of recognizing the trauma that we have all sustained while also helping us to focus on our shared and individual humanity."
- *Notes from the City*

104 Days of the Pandemic
© Copyright 2021 Daniel Damiano

All rights reserved. No part of this publication may be used or reproduced in any manner whatsoever without express written consent of the Author, with the exception of brief quotations embodied in critical articles or reviews.

Cover Design by DD Paint

Published by fandango 4 Art House (1st Edition)

ISBN: 978-0-578-97716-4

Poems

NYC, March 19th, 2020 – 11
Cabin Fever Blues - 12
Message in a Bottle - 13
You'll Go Blind, Otherwise - 14
The Toilet Paper Riots - 15
On Her 100th Birthday - 16
The Old Lambs - 17
The Daily Routine - 18
The Vast Indoor World - 19
On the Side of Caution - 20
The Art of the Bad Deal -21
The Helpful Ship - 22
Sunday Chores - 23
All Aboard the Insanity Train - 24
A Day Together - 26
Hope - 27
Your Anniversary - 28
Jamming in Heaven - 29
The Pillow Man - 30
Palm Sunday - 31
Awaiting the Twilight - 32
My Essential Wife - 33
Wyatt Earp Would Feel at Home - 34
The Odds - 35
The Sad Good Friday - 36
Easter Eve - 37
Easter Memory, or Sea Turtles - 38
And Then There Were 7 - 40
The Release of Paul Hildwin - 41

The Grand Scheme - 42
Thursday - 43
The Restless Natives - 44
Rainy Day - 45
Nothing is Immune - 46
What to Do - 47
Walls - 48
Broke - 49
How Far We've Come - 50
50,000 Plus Gone - 51
The Upside of America - 53
Gratitude from the Windows - 54
The Comfort of the Same - 55
Frontline Hero - 56
Remembering the Old Normal - 57
60,000 Plus Gone -58
A Boring Poem - 60
Rainy Day Fund Blues - 61
Ohio, 1970/2020 - 64
The Winged and the Whiskered - 65
A Visit to Greenwood Cemetery (Brooklyn, NY) - 66
70,000 Plus Gone - 67
Something - 69
The Last Run - 70
Alone but Not Alone yet Alone - 71
Mother's Day - 72
For a Friend Who Passed Away Today - 73
The Day After You Left Us - 74
Old Conga Drum - 75
80,000 Plus Gone -76

The Choice - 78
Tempus Fugit - 79
May Fools - 80
90,000 Plus Gone - 81
Parakeet White and Blue - 83
The Days in Between - 84
The Storm and the Calm - 85
Since These Times - 86
After This - 87
Welcome to the World - 88
100,000 Plus Gone - 89
You Needn't Believe - 91
7PM - 92
Minneapolis - 93
Knowing - 95
A State of Vertigo - 96
A Sort of Osmosis - 98
City of Wooden Canvases - 99
If... - 100
Voices in the Streets - 101
The First Deathless Day in New York City - 102
In Whitefish, Montana... - 103
Lockdown: A Social Media Thread - 104
Action - 105
Phase 1 - 106
Memories of Tiananmen Square - 107
A Greater Part - 108
Akin to Thornton Wilder - 110
"Karen" in Wisconsin - 111
Campaign of Ashes - 112
Supply and Demand - 113

The Birds - 114
Green - 115
A Not Quite Haiku - 116
Juneteenth - 117
A Civil Emergency - 118
Father's Day, Part II - 120
On Sweltering Summer Nights - 121
Of Magritte Proportions - 122
The Harder They Fall - 123
4am, on 45th - 124
Be Still, She Says - 125
Independence Day - 126
Still in the Woods - 127
18 Years - 128
104 Days of the Pandemic,
or Happy Birthday to Me - 129

The Why of This

I'll go out on a limb here and say that 2020 was a bit of an historical year; unfortunately, the majority of the reasons for that were by-and-large undesirable. But if you lived in the United States, or particularly in New York City, as my wife and I do, it was less historical than a complete and unequivocally radical immersion into a change in the way that we lived our lives. It changed not only life's barest simplicities, such as how we shopped for groceries or touched a doorknob, but also how we saw the world based on the actions or in-actions of our fellow citizens and governmental servants. From that came a bevy of discoveries that saw not only humanity at its worst but also heroism. It was also a year that stopped time and, for artists such as myself, it soon became clear that if I found time to write plays, poetry or a book in pre-pandemic life, the utter stoppage of the country and the world would offer little excuse to not do the same.

Beginning on March 19th, a week into our city's shutdown, an urge began for me to write a poem a day (if not more, should the inspiration arise) until my birthday (June 30th), which would serve to document this period. But this would not be relegated to the pandemic, as I might've initially presumed. It would also include personal poems that a particular day may have triggered. And as protests and violence and wrongful Covid-unrelated deaths surfaced, it would become something else again.

*For Judy
(My Essential Wife)*

NYC, March 19th, 2020
(3/19/20)

Travelling
to the city
on a largely vacant vessel
with a few masked riders,
above ground more of the same,
closings outnumbering openings,
gloves adorning hands,
masks over noses and mouths,
scarves over noses and mouths,
hoods over heads and noses,
zippers over mouths,
homeless men still opening
the few unlocked doors,
with so much space
between
all of this,
then back home,
captive to reportage,
the real and "fake" news,
as the numbers ascend
and toilet paper rolls decline
as grandeur deludes
and panics rise
and supplies fall
and leadership descends
and assurance wanes
as the world waits
…at a respectful distance.

Cabin Fever Blues
(3/20/20)

Will the lamps and windows
get bored with my tedium,
will they look at me as if I were a cat
struggling with the same mundane ball of yarn,
will the yawning ceiling look down on me
desperate for another character to enter this room,
will the medicine cabinet tell me to shave
after my whitened goat begins to upstage my chin,
will the toilet ask me to use the tub,
will the tub tell me I've showered enough,
will the fire escape try and lure me,
will my guitar gently weep
all over my conga drum,
all over the floor
and down the stairs
and through the door
and into the streets
where, one day,
I will breathe the outdoor air
and not have to think
twice?

Message in a Bottle
(3/21/20)

Last week you sent me your latest message,
as it'd been some time,
as it always is,
before I hear from you again,
now checking in because of *this*;
it always seems to take a tragedy,
aside from *our* tragedy,
but never when it's just Tuesday,
or Thursday
or any day that's just a day,
so I'll wait until the next event
to receive your message
washed ashore in the same old bottle
that rarely answers me.

You'll Go Blind, Otherwise
(3/22/20)

Turn away from the tangerine light,
who only tells us that all's well,
that there's a cure,
that supplies are there,
that his staff is flawless
and he more so,
and that it's China's fault.
Turn away from the tangerine light,
who shakes hands with devils,
ungloved
and unremorseful,
who spits his viral words
into the air
at the "terrible" throng
who questions his veneer.
Turn away from the tangerine light,
whose test came back so negative
that he's positive
that he's being portrayed negatively.
Turn away from the tangerine light,
and listen to those in labs,
in hospitals,
in clinics,
and all of those
who risk everything
in pursuit of the end
to this.

The Toilet Paper Riots
(3/23/20)

When the shit hits,
it does so literally,
judging from the salivating mobs
who clear the shelves,
leaving nothing but a pack of colored party napkins
and Dixie cups,
perhaps because the road to fear begins
and ends
in the same anatomical region;
when *War of the Worlds* was first broadcast on the radio,
it was said that the first thing the citizens did
was stock up on toilet paper,
no doubt in preparation for the expected anal-probings
from the unfriendly invaders
descending on the earth;
since then,
every panic and pandemic now leads
to the same grocery aisle,
where many a fatuous flock race
to embrace the Charmin,
its two-ply sheets now the crucifix that keeps
the natural and unnatural disasters
at bay.

On Her 100th Birthday
(3/24/20)

They gathered outside her room to wave at her,
she blew kisses through the window
and each child and grandchild
and niece and nephew
caught them like fireflies.
In turn, they blew their kisses back
louder and more animatedly
so that grandma's
hundred-year-old eyes
would see their affections,
hear their muffled declarations through the glass
and feel their embraces,
without the familiar warmth of their skin.

The Old Lambs
(3/24/20)

A lieutenant governor in Texas declares
that the geriocracy should sacrifice for the youth,
claiming that as a man of almost 70,
he too would brave the elements,
deny the mandated constraints
and, with suicidal abandon,
patronize restaurants,
bars, shops, malls, gyms,
disregarding the possible inhalation of contaminated air
for the sake of our economy.
He proclaims that they of grey hair
and creped skin have lived their best years,
but such lengths are necessary now,
their long lives having earned expendability,
but the children are our future
and they've gained the right to live beyond these days,
until they too become the old,
rife with knowledge of when they should waltz
into the next contagion,
like old lambs.

The Daily Routine
(3/25/20)

Create your makeshift burka
before venturing outside,
spray the door tongues and knobs as you leave,
walk the street
about six feet from the next cautious pedestrian,
and only handshake the air,
look carefully around you in the aisles
to make sure you're surrounded by the likeminded,
take your receipt with tweezers,
exchange muffled goodbyes
and swiftly depart,
spray the door tongues and knobs as you return,
shed your clothes like a cobra's skin,
immerse your hands in hot soap,
spray your clothes in a vodka/water mixture
(imbibe the remains),
then wait and wash your shirt and jeans
dangling in the sunlight
until dry.

The Vast Indoor World
(3/25/20)

At over 30,000 cases now,
we are the unequivocal epicenter
of this thing,
waiting on some vaporous cavalry's arrival;
if essential,
we work,
if non-essential,
we're broke
and waiting for the relief checks to arrive,
while the suits sit on their proposed figures
and debate into the needless nights.
We work, we wait, we look for work, we wait,
and wait for our loved ones to return from work,
and rinse their clothes and themselves
before we kiss.
We receive employment listings
for the same minimum wage jobs
in unprotected warehouses,
all run by the same svelte Daddy Warbucks clone,
because illness is in fashion
and they're dropping like infected flies
but someone needs to pack these many, many boxes
and ship them to the vast indoor world
that has little more to do
than wait and wait
and wait…

On the Side of Caution
(3/26/20)

We give the requisite six feet on either side
to allow our germs to descend unimpeded to the floor.
Despite the modest numbers,
the grocery store seems near-capacity,
extending a line of a masked 20 from checkout
through the frozen *Stouffer*'s and *Birdseye*,
past the perpetually vacant toilet paper aisle,
past the pork loins and almond milk,
all the way to the staff punch-out clock,
while scarved mouths muffle "Credit!"
to the cashiers resembling ER nurses,
making sure no one gets too close
to anything
but their own eggs.

The Art of the Bad Deal
(3/27/20)

Ventilators are doled out at a snail's pace
courtesy of the spray-tanned blackjack dealer
who barely gives credence
to the need for breath;
slowly and slowly, they eventually arrive
along with the masks, the gloves,
the respirators,
pushed down the Hudson
in a few wooden canoes
coasting on molasses.
Each day, as cases ascend,
the pace slackens to a crawl;
slower and slower, they come;
the masks, the gloves,
the respirators, the ventilators,
but the dealer withholds the oars
and sulks in his big white casino,
as bandanas make bandits of physicians
and other dying countries offer their help,
their money,
and, in an instant,
the United States has become a member
of the Third World.

The Helpful Ship
(3/28/20)

With its red cross emblazoned on its tall face,
and its imposing white metal body
wrapped around its innards of a thousand beds,
8 intensive care unit beds, 12 operating rooms,
4 radiology suites, 1200 navy medical personnel
and 70 civil service mariners,
the 70,000 ton *USNS Comfort*
departs comfortably enough today from Norfolk,
pushed off by "hope" and "solidarity"
before it's Monday arrival at Pier 90
in a most *un*comfortable New York City,
that waits and waits
as it works and works
to be saved.

Sunday Chores
(3/29/20)

I pick up the laundry,
then venture to the grocery store,
the steam from my covered nose and mouth fogs up my glasses
as I navigate the aisles for coffee, milk, sugar
and other household essentials.
I continually wipe my lenses,
so as to avoid tripping over small unmasked children,
and navigate back out to the streets.
With an overflowing single paper bag of items,
my glasses steam again,
and it's now like walking through a London fog,
my vision becoming increasingly impaired
with every step,
but soon I embrace my fading sense of sight,
the other masked pedestrians
and bleak Sunday silence
that now is our every day
fade out of my thinning path,
the wet sidewalk
gently slapped by the rain,
a rare passing car,
everything else
so quiet,
leading to my steps,
my red door,
my Brooklyn home.

All Aboard the Insanity Train
(3/30/20)

Look down at your wrist and see
what your id has wrought,
your ratings are up because there is little choice
but to watch your daily train descend off the rails
and crash into the fathomless ditch
of your own digging,
as you deflect the "fake" media
that is less interested in your numbers
than the dying,
and only return calls of red state governors
who would rather discuss the 8th hole on the green
than any states that are blue,
and coast on the helpful ship
that you were coerced to send
which arrived in our Harbor today
pushed to us with your closed arms
and Mussolini grin,
and let Easter be the symbol
of our economy's resurrection,
as the growing dead feel otherwise.
Our hope now lies in your embrace
of the shining moment
that is bereft of you,
when you heed the advice
of the true sages
and step away from the dais,
rest your fingers,
your tongue,
your hair,
and look down at your wrist
and know
that this
will forever be
on
your

watch.

A Day Together
(3/31/20)

On our day together,
my veiled wife and I dare
to visit our neighborhood's essential places:
the pharmacy for rubbing alcohol and sanitizer,
the grocery store for bags of cheap rigatoni,
peanut butter, bread and darling clementines,
the liquor store for pinot noir and tequila,
the deli for sandwiches and ginger ales,
then back to our apartment
to sterilize, eat
and breathe freely,
as we await the latest
from the governor.

Hope
(4/1/20)

With case numbers rising,
life remains at a standstill,
income flow all but a drip
as the discharged rejoice
and many die alone,
as weeks continue,
and creations and diversions are our savior,
earning like and love symbols,
a momentary satiation
that fails to pay the rent,
yet pushes the minutes by
through the wetness and grayness of recent days,
but today we are somehow warmed
by the sun's return
through the predominate clouds,
celestial and asking for our smiles,
and with it,
as always,
comes
a sort of hope.

Your Anniversary
(4/2/20)

Six years ago today
we saw you caged and waiting,
though it seemed as if you were the judge
of who best could whisk you away,
you of around 6 months
were rescued by nuns
and given the name "Chickapoo",
which we changed in a breath to Chula,
because you were unquestionably that,
as well as the thousand other names
we've given you since
as you traipse around the floors
undaunted
and perpetually curious,
in search of a new high shelf
or hidden enclave
or warm radiator
or sun-soaked windowsill,
until the front door opens
and you seize the moment
to claw at the hallway carpet
while batting your eyelashes with devilish joy,
and hoping the forbidden basement door is ajar
so that you can feel the 100-year old ghosts
that reside there
before fleeing back upstairs,
coerced by a balled-up receipt in our pockets,
and now we see you more than ever,
which you don't seem to mind,
and neither do we,
for the world is an ocean now
and, for the moment,
we can't venture far beyond the waves,
but you make it easier
to stay.

Jamming in Heaven
(4/3/20)

Some sunshine has been lost
with the passing of the talented Mr. Withers,
not of this bastard thing,
but he is allowed to die of something else, of course,
as his final note played earlier this week,
one that will carry on as long
as the last note of his "Lovely Day",
but 81 years isn't enough,
and many others will attest to this,
other musical icons who have, in fact, succumb of late
to this bastard thing,
having lived a lesser number of years,
halted careers that had not willfully ended,
their expressions through brass, ivory and strings,
a gift left to many souls and ears
who heard their many notes over many years.
No doubt they would have enjoyed more time
between the measures,
the flats and the sharps
and the crescendos
that all reside within life's unpredictable ballad,
but, at least for a time,
they were here,
playing for us.

The Pillow Man
(4/4/20)

In the midst of this,
he was plucked from rural Mankato
and brought to the Rose Garden
to extol the virtues of the Orange Emperor,
a man who once inhaled white rocks and dust
before wiping his nose and seeing the light,
triumphing in slumber
by returning rest to the weary;
his invention,
applauded by many heads and necks,
built him into a mustached symbol
of the American dream,
catapulting him from a man of doubt
to the undoubted,
adoring God
and equating our leader to His son
who has returned weeks before his resurrection,
and so now,
in the midst of our great pandemic,
the Pillow Man speaks to the country,
reading off a trembling piece of windblown notebook paper
how "grace" was restored on November 8th, 2016,
trumpeting needless pre-COVID numbers
while omitting the death tolls,
the new cases, the quarantines,
as his Jesus stands five feet behind him,
grinning at the memories,
before a good night's sleep.

Palm Sunday
(4/5/20)

We're told the apex is imminent,
          any day,
this week or next,
          more cases, more deaths,
more lack of what can save,
          which will only incur
more cases, more deaths,
          though some still gather in houses of worship,
where even God may not be now.

Awaiting the Twilight
(4/6/20)

It's as though 102 years ago were yesterday,
given what they said then
and say now,
to conceal our mouths,
avoid crowds,
insulate, isolate;
when the first World War was in its twilight,
after *Birth of a Nation* was screened
at his white house,
Woodrow took ill of the misnomered flu
while negotiating for peace,
as over a half-million Americans perished,
over 20 million in the world,
with much blame
aimed
at the Iberian Peninsula,
the "Spanish" source,
though never proven;
its origin aside,
many died,
as they do today,
as we conceal our mouths,
avoid crowds,
insulate, isolate
and await
the twilight.

My Essential Wife
(4/7/20)

Many of her days now
are spent
behind a plexiglass wall,
shielding her
from expelling tenants;
declared essential by the state,
she surfs on the largely vacant train,
often before dawn's break,
from Brooklyn to Manhattan,
masked and gloved
among other masked and gloved
or unmasked and unwise;
upon her arrival,
she becomes the lovely, anonymous glue
for many
who can do little without her,
and when she comes home
on the largely vacant train,
from Manhattan to Brooklyn,
masked and gloved,
among other masked and gloved
or unmasked and unwise,
she discards the day and the clothes
in the hallway
like a lizard's skin,
sanitizes and rinses
before our safe evening embrace
in the kitchen.

Wyatt Earp Would Feel at Home
(4/8/20)

I've returned to the ghost town
that is now
Manhattan,
and swear I can hear tumbleweeds barrel down the avenue,
resembling a metropolitan Tombstone
from Wyatt Earp's era;
on every corner is someone armed,
a policeman,
a soldier,
masked but with serious eyes,
as if awaiting a visible enemy at high noon;
every block is bare with possibilities,
a contrast to the clutter that
up until March 12th,
had been omnipresent;
without a badge or a gun,
I'm one of a few enigmas
who walk with a seeming destination;
without words, I'm asked why I'm there,
as it doesn't feel right to be out
among a town now run by the pigeons,
regardless of the unseasonable warmth,
the welcoming sun;
it is all far too quiet,
except for the sound of window shutters
opening and slamming closed,
like the moments before a duel.

The Odds
(4/9/20)

His gloveless hand caresses the gouda,
his maskless mouth sighs
all over the freezer doors,
perhaps because they're out of fish sticks;
and at check-out,
he waits behind me,
social distancing by a nose hair,
sniffling his naked nostrils
over my shoulder
like a mucus-infused pendulum
swinging over its prey,
before I turn to him
and through my mask, muffle,
"There's a virus going around,
in case you haven't caught the news",
and then it dawns on me,
in his prideful silence,
that he may not have heard,
and so who am I to judge
when we're just over a month in,
with over 5,000 deaths in our city,
with over 7,000 deaths in our state,
with over 16,000 deaths in our country,
with 82,837 in our world,
how should I expect him to possess
such clandestine knowledge
that I've somehow come upon,
when all this customer probably wants
is to not be impositioned
by this strange masked man

…who got the last box of fish sticks.

The Sad Good Friday
(4/10/20)

They were sailed to Hart's Island where,
after weeks of being unclaimed,
they were interred amidst
too many others;
the unnamed.

Easter Eve
(4/11/20)

Quiet pairs of feet shuffle outside
every blue moon,
sparrow chirps assert themselves
over sporadic engine clangs,
doorbell rings from cautious deliveries
occasionally intercede
on this eve
of a sad anniversary
that occurred 21 years ago tomorrow,
taking precedence over the Resurrection;
the still echoing voices
of my small family's demise,
reverberating beyond decibels
every year
at around this time.

Easter Memory, or Sea Turtles
(4/12/20)

With all due respect to Jesus,
this day has not exactly exclaimed rebirth to me,
not because I once ate an overdone ham in His honor,
or because I was traumatized at a young age
by an Easter egg hunt gone awry,
or because Catholic school was a horror
and the uniforms were tight,
but for reasons I can barely remember now;
ones that, nevertheless,
were the entrée of a particular Easter gathering
21 years ago today,
which was consumed with my Grandmother's finest silverware
until the forks were dropped
and the knives wielded,
and then the end somehow came
and things would never be the same
again,
and since then
family has been a strange word to me;
thinking for much of my younger years
that we were tethered,
despite no shortage of the adverse,
that it was unwritten law
that bonded us,
and so trauma would be in our uncomposed contract
and the holidays would be the arena
in which ultimate battles reigned;
Thanksgiving, Christmas,
and, oh, Easter –
Easter, how you came to symbolize the worst of it,
which is not to question if Jesus returned,
or the sacredness of this day,
but there were other things that have occurred since,
and this was one of them

though it matters to so very few,
but I'm among them
and this is what I know,
what I've known,
what I've worked through
and what will be with me,
and there's a lesson here
immersed deep in life's wet sand
that takes one years to excavate with bare hands,

but the gist is that
young sea turtles have to find their own way
to the ocean,
so what's *our* excuse?
And so we move on,
now washing lemon rinds in the sink
as cathedral bells ring
for a mass of the unseen,
with many having their own memories of this day,
some much better than mine,
some far worse,
some may also die on this day,
while others may recover
and go on to reflect on how close they were
to never celebrating Easter
again.

And Then There Were 7
(4/13/20)

…waiting for the green flag
to fall from the emperor's lawn,
because Lemmon, South Dakota
and Little Rock, Arkansas
and Provo, Utah
and Omaha, Nebraska
and Cheyenne, Wyoming
and Des Moines, Iowa
and Bizmarck, North Dakota

"aren't New York City",

so why shouldn't their citizens roam free
and in herds
and ignore the rest of our Rome
that still burns?

The Release of Paul Hildwin
(4/14/20)

Welcome home, Paul Hildwin,
you've been away so long,
35 years in a box with bars,
while singing your innocence song.

Welcome home, Paul Hildwin,
apologies for your sentences to death,
from way back in 1986,
when you took your last free breath.

Welcome home, Paul Hildwin,
you're a free man at a cost,
now Social security is all you get
along with memories of 35 years lost.

Welcome home, Paul Hildwin,
you've endured more than words can say,
2 death sentences, 3 cancer bouts
and yet here you are today.

Welcome Home, Paul Hildwin,
your release was not foreseen,
now freedom's come with open arms to you,

except…now you're quarantined.

The Grand Scheme
(4/15/20)

But, of course, wrestling has been declared "essential"
in the Orange State,
and, of course, its president has been appointed
as an adviser to the Orange Emperor,
and, of course, many still think this pandemic is a ruse,
designed solely to make us impoverished
and keep us out of Dairy Queens,
and, of course, this has prompted a quaking surge
of unmasked protests in the town squares,
and, of course, this massive ploy has been etched by scientists
who, of course, have invested shares
in this national nadir
who, of course, have feigned a vaccine's creation
that is likely a mere sedative designed to send us to slumber
for the absconsion of our wallets,
whose audacious warnings for citizens
to remain in their domestic lairs, can
of course, be attributed to nothing more
than a diversionary tactic
for doctors and nurses
looking to pillage the garden gnomes
and plum tomatoes from America's front lawns,
while the sheltered souls remain in their dens,
none the wiser
to this grand scheme.

Thursday
(4/16/20)

Let it just be Thursday
and try not to attach strings,
let it just be Thursday
without the anxiety of the unknown,
let it just be Thursday
and bring in the laundry and make scrambled eggs for breakfast,
let it just be Thursday
and strum the guitar and let the cat gnaw on your finger,
let it just be Thursday
and let the squirrels on the fire escape be your television,
let it just be Thursday
without anger,
without frustration,
without the compulsion to caterwaul to the sky,
let it just be Thursday
without a thought to Friday
or Saturday
or Sunday
or Monday
or Tuesday
or Wednesday
or the summer,
or autumn,
or the holiday season,
let it just be today
and sit with the minutes
and the remaining hours
that crawl and fly at once
like a sloth with wings
that doesn't even care
what day this is.

The Restless Natives
(4/17/20)

The 2nd amendment now stokes the fire,
in Lansing and Columbus and elsewhere, their ire
usurps the strategies on how best to survive,
now all they see is how they've been deprived,
as the mobs scream through the glass panes of statehouse doors;
they'll be damned if they'll be protected anymore.

Rainy Day
(4/18/20)

Rain falls against the window
this Saturday afternoon,
and the feathered are under awnings
and the squirrels are in their trees
waiting for the clearing,
as we are.

Nothing is Immune
(4/19/20)

In Athens, they disinfect the statue of Pericles,
who perished in a forgotten plague;
it seems even his white Carrara marble
can no longer protect him these days.

What To Do
(4/20/20)

I could write about protesting Americans
unbridled in their pursuit of liberty and death,
or I can opt to describe how two doves
ate seeds from the troth on our fire escape
while our wide-eyed cat gurgled
before ceasing their festivities,
or I can note the anniversary
of the modestly-famed rabbit attack
on President Jimmy Carter,
on this day in 1979,
…
or I can just scrap this poem
altogether.

Walls
(4/21/20)

They will not be the cure
for the many current ills,
they will not provide jobs
or pay the many bills
of any of the defiant, railing in the streets,
flexing their magazines, stomping their feet;
they will not be a solution,
be it the final or the first,
they will be only smoke and mirrors
used to mask the viral burst.

Broke
(4/23/20)

Oh, stimulus, stimulus –
the pittance to survive,
for the umpteenth day I've waited
and you've yet to arrive.
Unemployment, Unemployment –
the dangling carrot's yet to fall,
the credit cards are maximized,
and now we're waiting for it all.

How Far We've Come
(4/22/20)

A half century ago
the earth was celebrated,
its littered streets and smog-filled skies
and contaminated waters
and the extinct and nearly-extinct species
were paraded through towns and cities,
as if to say *"Look at what we've done"*,
and the day became annually adored,
and bills were passed,
for water,
for air,
for animals,
but things somehow continued;
Iron Eyes Cody still cried for years,
and 50 Earth Days later
we have eroding glaciers,
contaminated water,
littered streets, smog-filled skies,
extinct and nearly-extinct species,
signatures etched and erased,
and now protests parading downtown,
or in the town square,
or town halls, or townships
spouting how their freedom extends
to their right to shun heed
while shooting blindly
at an unseen enemy,
as the clouds peer down,
squinting through the ozone hole,
as if to say
"Look at what you've done."

50,000 Plus Gone
(4/24/20)

Grandfathers, grandmothers,
fathers, mothers,
sons, daughters,
uncles, aunts,
nieces, nephews,
cousins, friends,
employees, employers,
vendors, volunteers,
doctors, nurses,
in Alabama, Alaska,
Arizona, Arkansas,
California, Colorado,
Connecticut, Delaware,
the District of Columbia,
Florida, Georgia, Hawaii,
Idaho, Illinois, Indiana, Iowa,
Kansas, Kentucky,
Louisiana, Maine, Maryland,
Massachusetts, Michigan,
Minnesota, Mississippi,
Missouri, Montana,
Nebraska, Nevada,
New Hampshire, New Jersey,
New Mexico, New York,
North Carolina, North Dakota,
Ohio, Oklahoma, Oregon,
Pennsylvania, Rhode Island,
South Carolina, South Dakota,
Tennessee, Texas,
Utah, Vermont, Virginia,
Washington, West Virginia,
Wisconsin, Wyoming,
Guam, Mariana Islands,
Puerto Rico, the Virgin Islands…

not to mention
the rest
of
this
beautiful
world.

The Upside of America
(4/25/20)

The governor of New York
received a letter from a retired Kansas farmer,
"You're very busy during this time,
but I'm sending you a mask
for a doctor or nurse there";
this from a family of four
with a fifth mask to spare,
this from a husband
with a wife with one functioning lung,
this from a man who may've never been to New York,
who may've looked at it as another world,
as many in this country do,
but he saw no difference;
he only knew that one mask
could come in handy.

Gratitude from the Windows
(4/26/20)

Descending but with caution,
the New York numbers go down,
though the feet remain on the pedal,
the prayers and chants and vibes
continue to permeate the air,
the pots and pans bang and clang,
igniting the healthcare parades at 7pm,
through every borough
the songs continue,
the bare-palmed applause makes
an award-ceremony of myriad avenues,
as the masked white and powder blue garbed
wave and weep
from the city streets
each and every day,
knowing that this thankful cacophony
will not cease
until this dark cloud
has faded
into the blue.

The Comfort of the Same
(4/27/20)

Gray skies overhead
with casserole fumes from the oven
wafting past the cat on the couch arm
tanning under the Tiffany lamp,
the low tide sounds
of faraway cars on the Gowanus,
masked deliveries of Mexican food on wheels
and down and uphill treks
to and from the 45th Street subway station
from my window
        from my window
                from my window…

Frontline Hero
(4/28/20)

Behind the mask
and the blue scrubs
and the form-fitting gloves
and the plastic-covered shoes
was a heart
shattered like many recurring mirrors
from the perishing onslaught
in such a narrow window
of time,
and it didn't matter
the degrees she amassed,
the honors bestowed,
the respect incurred;
in the end,
she simply could not be expected
to not be

human.

Remembering the Old Normal
(4/30/20)

We hear the clichés now,
how it took such a thing as this
to connect to each other,
even though just prior
we had phones suctioned to our palms,
and wrote novels to each other with our thumbs,
and were courageously indignant
with capital letters and exclamations,
and had our heads down,
as if in prayer
for the next viral sensation,
never fathoming the next one would be a virus,
so now we Facetime or Skype or Zoom
or any other methods sure to be antiquated
in a few years,
and hear the forgotten cadences
of our friends
and relatives
and wonder
how long we can sustain such exchanges
before the Pavlovian ding
pulls us back
to the old normal.

60,000 Plus Gone
(4/30/20)

Grandfathers, grandmothers,
fathers, mothers,
sons, daughters,
uncles, aunts,
nieces, nephews,
cousins, friends,
employees, employers,
vendors, volunteers,
doctors, nurses,
in Alabama, Alaska,
Arizona, Arkansas,
California, Colorado,
Connecticut, Delaware,
the District of Columbia,
Florida, Georgia, Hawaii,
Idaho, Illinois, Indiana, Iowa,
Kansas, Kentucky,
Louisiana, Maine, Maryland,
Massachusetts, Michigan,
Minnesota, Mississippi,
Missouri, Montana,
Nebraska, Nevada,
New Hampshire, New Jersey,
New Mexico, New York,
North Carolina, North Dakota,
Ohio, Oklahoma, Oregon,
Pennsylvania, Rhode Island,
South Carolina, South Dakota,
Tennessee, Texas,
Utah, Vermont, Virginia,
Washington, West Virginia,
Wisconsin, Wyoming,
Guam, Mariana Islands,
Puerto Rico, the Virgin Islands…

not to mention
the rest
of
this
beautiful
world.

A Boring Poem
(5/1/20)

When folding laundry becomes a thrill,
when buttered toast is living on the edge,
when a broken street-lamp spawns intrigue,
when a masked man
scratching Pick-6 tickets under your window
leaves you hoping that he will pirouette at the results,
when a police siren makes you ponder,
when an ambulance makes you stop folding your laundry
and ultimately lulls you to sleep,
where you dream of buttered toast.

Rainy Day Fund Blues
(5/2/20)

They say to have 3 months saved up
for a "rainy day",
but try doing that in New York City
as a freelance artist
or in America
as pretty much anything;
"but you should've been prepared for such a catastrophe",
ah, yes,
we of little income should've had peripheral vision
when our government was blindsided;
"you should've worked a 9-5 office job";
ah, yes,
I've done that as well,
watched myself atrophy behind a desk,
sat beside banal personalities
whose cultural net
barely extended beyond *Aqua Man*,
including the one guy from New Jersey
who thought Trump was "honest",
and the CEOs and CFOs who never said hello
or blessed your sneeze
but extended the occasional Pizza Friday
as unspoken compensation
for how the insurance
inhaled most of our salaries;
they say *"you should've saved up beginning in high school",*
ah, yes,
says a man who retired at 24
who, when asked how he managed this,
says that he never went out,
not for dinner,
nor for a movie,
and now deprives his wife and children
of the same simple life luxuries,
and used part of his financial aid to buy a house,

where he rents out rooms
to suckers who haven't saved up 3 months
in case of a "rainy day";
they say *"you shouldn't overindulge"*,
ah, yes,
so I guess I should pull back
on my bi-weekly bagel and butter at *Sunset Bagels*,
or monthly pepperoni slice at *Luigi's*
or bi-monthly .99 cent song download,
but then there's still the rent,
the electric,
the cell phone,
the credit cards
the cat food,
our food,
not to mention a few previous "rainy days"
that tend to creep up on many an American life:
9/11, the financial crisis, hospitalizations,
the many natural and unnatural disasters
void of fiscal sympathies,
but we should *still* have 3 months saved up
for a "rainy day",
ah, yes,
a day which has become many days,
now casting its foreboding clouds over a month
and soon two
and eventually three -
now there's *no* income,
and the government thinks sending a check is a gratuity
for checking their coats,
…
so now what?;
ah, yes,
our parents,
many of whom are dead or estranged
or living in tiny apartments
or barely surviving off a pittance from Social Security
with little to no savings

or who already have one of our siblings in their old room
with a perpetually unleashed pitbull named "Sweety Pie"
just waiting for the opportunity
to eat our eyeballs as we sleep;
ah, yes,
there's always
the woods,
that is
until
the wolves and possum
arrive at our makeshift door
and chase us back
to a home
we can never go back to
again,
as we circle aimlessly,
awaiting the rainbow.

Ohio, 1970/2020
(5/3/20)

---

50 years ago today
67 shots were heard around the world,
as students adorned the lawns of Kent State
in protest of a lawless war,
immune to the naysayers
and Nixon,
who called them "bums",
tear gas filled the air
as the anti-war voices punched through the mist,
undeterred by the cross hairs they were now in
by the army of National Guardsmen
on the other side of the green,
the fire of this stoked by a president immune to guilt
who waited for a vaporous victory,
before the bullets let their presence be known
and reduced peace to lifeless bodies,
and today statehouses are raided
with civilians in the role of the National Guard,
armed with exposed mouths
and assault rifles,
and governors and staff wear bulletproof vests
and police stand before them,
inhaling the toxic breath of the raging ammo-clad,
the fire of this stoked by a president immune to guilt,
who waits for a vaporous victory,

    before the bullets let their presence be known.

The Winged and the Whiskered
(5/4/20)

They descend below the morning kitchen window,
sampling seeds from the fire escape buffet,
just under the inhospitable eyes
of our whiskered one
whose ears press against the screen
in an attempt to disturb the festivities,
her sporadic throat-tremors prompt the feathered
to occasionally river dance along the metal slats
before soft-shoeing back to the feast,
nibbling, cooing
and shaking their talons
victoriously.

A Visit to Greenwood Cemetery (Brooklyn, NY)
(5/5/20)

Surrounded by the peaceful resting,
old granite stones display the lifespan of those who lived
so long ago
revealing the brevity of their time,
a 6 year-old son in the late 1800s,
a 10 year-old daughter at the turn of the century,
other children whose lives ended before they began,
so many so young,
so many older but not old,
so few who lived to be old
make up a part of this centuries-old solitude
that may be the safest place in our world.

70,000 Plus Gone
(5/6/20)

Grandfathers, grandmothers,
fathers, mothers,
sons, daughters,
uncles, aunts,
nieces, nephews,
cousins, friends,
employees, employers,
vendors, volunteers,
doctors, nurses,
in Alabama, Alaska,
Arizona, Arkansas,
California, Colorado,
Connecticut, Delaware,
the District of Columbia,
Florida, Georgia, Hawaii,
Idaho, Illinois, Indiana, Iowa,
Kansas, Kentucky,
Louisiana, Maine, Maryland,
Massachusetts, Michigan,
Minnesota, Mississippi,
Missouri, Montana,
Nebraska, Nevada,
New Hampshire, New Jersey,
New Mexico, New York,
North Carolina, North Dakota,
Ohio, Oklahoma, Oregon,
Pennsylvania, Rhode Island,
South Carolina, South Dakota,
Tennessee, Texas,
Utah, Vermont, Virginia,
Washington, West Virginia,
Wisconsin, Wyoming,
Guam, Mariana Islands,
Puerto Rico, the Virgin Islands…

not to mention
the rest
of
this
beautiful
world.

Something
(5/7/20)

I've had a migraine for much of this day,
and it was all that I could do,
with three minutes left of this Thursday night,
to write something to you.

The Last Run
(5/8/20)

---

3 gunshots cracked along
a quiet road in the enclave of Satilla Shores,
as he lay there
gawked at by a smoking barrel
and a camera's eye
awaiting his death,
clad in only running shorts, a shirt and Nike sneakers,
the dispatch would ask over the phone
what he had done,
a voice replied
"It's kind of an ongoing thing out here",
which begs the question
of what "thing" that could be,
when a man is armed only with his black skin
on an afternoon jog
where flowers now lay for him.

Alone but Not Alone yet Alone
(5/9/20)

―――――――――――――

I'm not alone in feeling restless,
I'm not alone in feeling alone,
I'm not alone in wanting to walk the streets with a naked face
I'm not alone in feeling alone,
I'm not alone in being wary of the unknown,
I'm not alone in feeling alone,
I'm not alone in seeking the light at the end of this,
I'm not alone in feeling alone,
I'm not alone in desiring more than voices and images,
I'm not alone in feeling alone,
I'm not alone in being enraged at the ignorant,
I'm not alone in feeling alone,
I'm not alone in wondering how things will change
I'm not alone in feeling alone,
I'm not alone in my sadness on this day and others,
I'm not alone in feeling alone;
and even if I was,
       there are worse things.

Mother's Day
(5/10/20)

Few things say this day
like reading Dostoyevsky
with your cat at your ottoman-raised feet
by your bay windows
that watch the row houses sunbathing
with their window eyes closed
as the street leaves quietly waft
and every creak in your old walls
prompts your cat's ears to antennas,
with not a mother in sight.

For a Friend Who Passed Away Today
(5/11/20 - for David Green)

The condolences and tributes
stream down unimpeded
like cascading water
this evening,
honoring our friend
who passed away from this bastard thing today,
a singer, an actor, a brother, an uncle,
a friend,
an Ohio thespian in the Garden State,
a spirit,
as the memories of many continue
their loving waterfall
which warmly paints his now memorial wall;
how one met him,
    where they performed,
        when they were in college,
            a video of a Carly Simon song he crooned,
                photos from the stage, in black & white and color,
the times that were had;
how stunned, how saddened
we all are
at how this worthy life was whisked away
today.

The Day After You Left Us
(5/12/20)

It makes me wonder
    what you see now.
It makes me hope with every fiber
    that all the consolations that often
        come with death
    are true;
a better place,
  one void of pain,
      a bliss
    unfathomable to us living.

Old Conga Drum
(5/13/20)

Today
I played you for the first time
in a while,
perhaps out of some sort of inanimate guilt,
since I rescued you from the curb
for a reason
a couple of summers ago,
and bandaged the hairline crack
along your wooden side;
you just looked too nice to me
to put out to pasture,
even if your tone is wanting now,
even if your response to my palms paradiddles
is *why bother?*

I know why.

80,000 Plus Gone
(5/14/20)

Grandfathers, grandmothers,
fathers, mothers,
sons, daughters,
uncles, aunts,
nieces, nephews,
cousins, friends,
employees, employers,
vendors, volunteers,
doctors, nurses,
in Alabama, Alaska,
Arizona, Arkansas,
California, Colorado,
Connecticut, Delaware,
the District of Columbia,
Florida, Georgia, Hawaii,
Idaho, Illinois, Indiana, Iowa,
Kansas, Kentucky,
Louisiana, Maine, Maryland,
Massachusetts, Michigan,
Minnesota, Mississippi,
Missouri, Montana,
Nebraska, Nevada,
New Hampshire, New Jersey,
New Mexico, New York,
North Carolina, North Dakota,
Ohio, Oklahoma, Oregon,
Pennsylvania, Rhode Island,
South Carolina, South Dakota,
Tennessee,
Texas,
Utah, Vermont, Virginia,
Washington, West Virginia,
Wisconsin, Wyoming,
Guam, Mariana Islands,
Puerto Rico, the Virgin Islands…

not to mention
the rest
of
this
beautiful
world.

The Choice
(5/15/17)

There's unity
and there's division -
both require effort.

Tempus Fugit
(5/16/20)

Days go by
like a finger snap,
from Monday's sun and blue
to Tuesday's overcasting
to Wednesday's precipitation
to Thursday's hail
to Friday's humidity
to Saturday's church bells
summoning God down
for Sunday dinner,
before He leaves in advance of the weekend rush
and the days continue in their unbroken stream,
as He binge-watches the world from above the sky,
aghast, amused, disheartened, dismayed
at all that he saw coming.

May Fools
(5/17/20)

They're there,
at least 1 of every 6
with mouths and nostrils unadorned
who walk the pavement and park paths
as foolish as an open bathrobe in winter,
and with May warmth
comes greater whim,
and with May sun
comes an increase in caprice
and with May heat,
the odds surge all the more
and favor the fools.

90,000 Plus Gone
(5/18/20)

Grandfathers, grandmothers,
fathers, mothers,
sons, daughters,
uncles, aunts,
nieces, nephews,
cousins, friends,
employees, employers,
vendors, volunteers,
doctors, nurses,
in Alabama, Alaska,
Arizona, Arkansas,
California, Colorado,
Connecticut, Delaware,
the District of Columbia,
Florida, Georgia, Hawaii,
Idaho, Illinois, Indiana, Iowa,
Kansas, Kentucky,
Louisiana, Maine, Maryland,
Massachusetts, Michigan,
Minnesota, Mississippi,
Missouri, Montana,
Nebraska, Nevada,
New Hampshire, New Jersey,
New Mexico, New York,
North Carolina, North Dakota,
Ohio, Oklahoma, Oregon,
Pennsylvania, Rhode Island,
South Carolina, South Dakota,
Tennessee, Texas,
Utah, Vermont, Virginia,
Washington, West Virginia,
Wisconsin, Wyoming,
Guam, Mariana Islands,
Puerto Rico, the Virgin Islands…

not to mention
the rest
of
this
beautiful
world.

Parakeet White and Blue
(5/19/20)

Gizmo had escaped,
because even a caged bird
can feel caged,
so out the window he flew
from his apartment at 22nd and 5th,
his owner pleading for the return
of her "Parakeet White & Blue",
as he circles the city,
dodges the street-smart sparrows and pigeons,
avoids their christened terrain
of sun-bleached branches and awnings,
rides atop an elevated R train,
pecks at sidewalk pepperoni shards,
dances along toasty windowsills,
before returning like a boomerang
to the source
of his captivity,
his unlatched cage awaiting him,
his owner
not blaming him,
especially these days.

The Days in Between
(5/20/20)

Early morning Wednesday
my wife leaves for the city
before returning on Friday
and in the days between
the cat will be my shadow
in every room I enter
and she'll be on my lap
at the onset of my bent knees
and she'll meow a little bit more
and eat a little bit more
and every sound from the downstairs foyer
will be a possibility.

The Storm and the Calm
(5/21/20)

There's been little deviation
from this perpetually improvised script
despite the momentary masks and quarantine
and obsession with Clorox, swabs and antibodies,
because life has always been the great unknown,
maybe more so than what comes after,
clandestine,
lawless,
like waters idle for months
that one day
decide to level homes along the shore
before the calm returns.

Since These Times
(5/22/20)

Today was a surprise,
beginning with a half-eyed morning gander
at my bank account
that had come to resemble
a gradually draining pond,
now filled a bit
courtesy of the Department of Labor's reward
for my laborious efforts
to convey
that I wasn't working enough to live,
and so up until now
I shopped with handcuffs,
as my wife carried us
with her "essential" income
while friends who knew of our struggle
offered money,
which we loudly refused,
and now a part-time teaching gig,
an emergency grant
and a sudden if mild geyser
of backed-up unemployment benefits
have given breath
to pay the late rent,
pay the phone,
pay the credit card,
donate to the Blind Cat Sanctuary
of St. Pauls, North Carolina
in honor
of our recently deceased friend,
and regain a modicum
of respectability
for the first time
since
these times.

After This
(5/23/20)

What the after of this
will be
is as clear
as
a sojourn
through a cave at dusk
with an astigmatism
while wearing the prescription sunglasses
of a stranger.

Welcome to the World
(5/24/20)

The armada of cars
idle past our windows
with sputtering horns gently commanding attention,
teal and pink and green balloons weave and bob,
salutations on poster board
jutted through sun roofs,
It's a Boy in bright letters
on side windows,
welcoming the world's new addition
from afar.

100,000 Plus Gone
(5/25/20)

Grandfathers, grandmothers,
fathers, mothers,
sons, daughters,
uncles, aunts,
nieces, nephews,
cousins, friends,
employees, employers,
vendors, volunteers,
doctors, nurses,
in Alabama, Alaska,
Arizona, Arkansas,
California, Colorado,
Connecticut, Delaware,
the District of Columbia,
Florida, Georgia, Hawaii,
Idaho, Illinois, Indiana, Iowa,
Kansas, Kentucky,
Louisiana, Maine, Maryland,
Massachusetts, Michigan,
Minnesota, Mississippi,
Missouri, Montana,
Nebraska, Nevada,
New Hampshire, New Jersey,
New Mexico, New York,
North Carolina, North Dakota,
Ohio, Oklahoma, Oregon,
Pennsylvania, Rhode Island,
South Carolina, South Dakota,
Tennessee, Texas,
Utah, Vermont, Virginia,
Washington, West Virginia,
Wisconsin, Wyoming,
Guam, Mariana Islands,
Puerto Rico, the Virgin Islands…

not to mention
the rest
of
this
beautiful
world.

You Needn't Believe
(5/26/20)

…that America would halt
its epithetic tongue
or that wrongful deaths
would be suppressed
by an unseen enemy
that some fear
and others dismiss as a passing fad
while the chlorined pools summon the scantily clad;
after all,
the young, the middle-aged and the old
cannot die from the invisible,
or so they're told,
any more than
a black man can be murdered
for his blackness,
any more than a security guard can be murdered
for protecting,
any more than spin doctors
can veto doctors
so that waffles can be publicly consumed
without a second thought
to what still
is in the air.

7pm
(5/27/20)

If I lose myself in a day
and fail to glance at a clock,
I'll always know it's that time
by the first clang of a metal pot,
then frying pans, then cowbells,
then bongos and drums ensue,
then whistles and chimes join and harmonize
until approximately 7:02.

Minneapolis
(5/28/20)

Flames were fanned
in Minneapolis
last night,
and the vast history of civil unrest
wafted with the smoke and tear gas:
the Red Summer Riots of 1919,
the Tulsa Riots of '21,
the Perry Riots of '22,
the Watsonville Riot of '30,
the Detroit and Harlem Riots of '43,
the Cicero Riots of '51,
the Birmingham Riots of '63,
the Harlem and Rochester Riots of '64,
the Watts Riots of '65,
the Avondale, Buffalo, Cairo, Cambridge,
Milwaukee, Newark, Plainfield
and Saginaw Riots of '67,
the Akron, Avondale, Chicago, Detroit, Kansas City,
New York City, DC, Louisville, Miami, Pittsburgh,
Trenton and Wilmington Riots of '68,
the Stonewall Riots of '69,
the Augusta and Asbury Park Riots of '70,
the Boston Busing Riot of '74,
Tompkins Square Park in '88,
Miami in '89,
DC and Crown Heights in '91,
the Rodney King riots of '92,
the Oakland Riots of '14,
and so on…
but the maskless, the armed and the white
can storm a statehouse
and not be gassed,
and not be shot,
and a white man
can try and pass a fake $20 bill

in Minneapolis
and not think
the penalty

will be death.

Knowing
(5/29/20)

---

looking outside
at the cooing doves
who look back at me,
knowing everything.

A State of Vertigo
(5/31/20)

At 4pm on Friday,
everything was spinning,
as I rode the train into the city,
my equilibrium
radically unequal,
as the heat from my mask
and gloves
rendered beads of sweat,
yet still managing
to request that a sneezing woman
kindly
cover her mouth,
as she walked by
in her oblivious summer dress,
and at my arrival home
I abruptly crashed,
dead to the world
as the country mourned the dead,
and on Saturday night
I shakily woke,
my head still a'twirl,
as was the country,
city by city,
tremoring with grief
and anger
as our Finest braced themselves,
some better than others,
and the National Guard was brought in,
and eyes were being quenched with milk,
and history was recurring
before *my* eyes,
a flashback to times
in my lifetime
and before it,
the well-meaning poster board signs

and pleas
trying to outnumber
the empty-handed,
who may not even know who George Floyd is or was,
as leadership grasps at straws
in hopes that our fearful leader's
venomous tongue
will remain silent,
as the next night is just hours away
and we hope,
I hope,
we all should hope
that peace transcends,
that words are the action
and not the hurls of tear gas
and lethal cocktails
that will only keep this country
in a state
of vertigo.

A Sort of Osmosis
(6/2/20)

Monday brought with it
a sort of osmosis,
my throbbing temple
and continued imbalance
conjoined
with the continued imbalance
shaking the temple
and the many cities
through many states,
while the Orange Emperor waltzes
down a teargassed path
to the diocese,
brandishing a bible
like a cannon
aimed squarely at
this country.

City of Wooden Canvases
(6/3/20)

The dawn of a new
New York City day
brings with it
newly erected walls
over easels of unshattered windows
where, not long ago,
our masked reflections
were once seen,
now these wooden canvases
exclaim
in black and red spray paint,
as if from a screaming mouth -
Amerika was never great!

If...
(6/4/20)

If I believe in good,
then I believe in humanity,
in peace
and love
and an end of an era as a beginning,
and a beginning as possibility,
like when an illness fades
with the dead
and the spirit ascends,
having left its lesson plan behind
for our perusal
in the hopes
that
with new life
comes
a kind of
epiphany.

Voices in the Streets
(6/5/20)

Humid rain
washes the tension
from the streets
around
the evening city,
everything else remains
like an adhesive against the pavement
where many feet have gathered nightly
at Atlantic Ave,
in Jackson Heights,
in Union Square,
in midtown,
the Bronx,
with hoisted posters
dried and dampened,
held high
between the wooden boards
of the many markets and stores,
with cries that reverberate off the clouds
with the cries from Minneapolis,
Chicago, Seattle, Philadelphia,
Miami, Los Angeles, Buffalo,
Rochester, Atlanta, Detroit...

"What do we want? Justice!"

"When do we want it? Now!"

The First Deathless Day in New York City
(6/5/20)

A deathless day
has finally come,
to the city so used
to an adverse sum:
no, Corona, you've escorted enough
to the blinding light,
may it end in perpetuity,
your fatal blight.
Go away, be gone,
you sinister cells,
let the recovering recover,
let them taste, let them smell.
May death from you end
on this day and beyond,
may all the filled lungs clear,
may this interminable battle be done.

*It was initially reported by some news sources that June 5th was the first day of no reported Covid-related death in NYC. This, unfortunately, was later proven not to be the case. It was then reported that July 11th was actually the first day of no reported Covid-related deaths in the city. As of this writing, it is uncertain if even that is accurate.

In Whitefish, Montana…
(6/6/20)

---

he circled like a bull
spouting
to the masked throng
who only wanted black lives to matter;
with every "Fuck You" he bellowed,
they replied "Peaceful!",
"Fuck You!",
"Peaceful!",
as he continued to navigate
through the chorus of undeterred voices,
waiting for the excuse to charge
with his horns aimed,
but they refused
to display the red cape
to him
or any sword
beneath.

Lockdown: A Social Media Thread
(6/7/20)

Him: They need to end this lockdown.
Me: Well, one step at a time. Phase 1 is tomorrow.
Him: They should've ended it 3 weeks ago when the curve flattened.
Me: Well, there were still cases and deaths.
Him: I just think it's all moot now. The curve was flattened.
Me: But there were still cases and deaths.
Him: I'm just saying, they gave us enough rules. And now we have these protests with thousands of people walking side by side and not taking any precautions.
Me: Okay, so what are you saying?
Him: I'm just saying this has been overdue.
Me: The protests?
Him: No, the lockdown.
Me: Okay, so you're saying the lockdown needs to end even though we now have protests, which you think will prolong the virus and possibly send us back to a lockdown?
Him: I'm saying these protests consist of people who aren't wearing masks and social distancing, so what's the point in anyone following these rules?
Me: Well, we can still be individually responsible. I mean, this isn't the flu. This can re-occur in August, and then we'll have to lock everything down again.
Him: That's my point.
Me: What…is?
Him: They should've ended the lockdown already.
Me: But…even if they ended the lockdown 3 weeks ago, George Floyd would've still died and we would still have had these protests. So I'm not quite clear on your point. I mean, are you saying all this to justify not wearing a mask and social distancing?
Him: …No.
Me: Are you not wearing a mask and social distancing?
Him: …
Me: Hello?

Action
(6/8/20)

The night wafts in
like confusion,
humid
with an ulterior motive;
it wants something
from me,
other than
nocturnal
musing.

Phase 1
(6/8/20)

Non-essentials
can now come and go
like a masked breeze
on the trains and streets and stores,
almost like in the old halcyon days,
before March 12th,
but caution infuses the air,
despite the sun and smiling sky,
and whispers
"don't think
the worst
can't return."

Memories of Tiananmen Square
(6/9/20)

They tried,
symbolic in that unnamed man
standing before a certain death
only to live
and live on,
then fading into the unknown annals
of history,
as if born only
for anonymous martyrdom,
the symbol
of inspiration,
if not victory,
to other countries
who heard the cries
and yielded,
but not China then,
nor China now,
who look out
at the new faceless and nameless,
unborn 31 years ago
but alive today
to raise their fists
and resurrect
the unknown man
who pitted his flesh
against communist steel,
and, in the end,
there is a victory
in that.

A Greater Part
(6/11/20)

I was born into the grass and cement
of a small Jersey town
that didn't look much different from me;
working-class Italian, Irish, German and Polish names
ubiquitous on mailboxes,
where fatherlessness
was the trend,
as our working single mothers
commuted here and there
from job to job to job,
sometimes drinking too much,
sometimes angry too much,
and us sons and daughters grew up early,
making our own eggs and toast,
working paper routes
and dishwashing
and snow-shoveling
and raking leaves
and picking tomatoes
or retrieving golf balls at driving ranges
in fear for our lives,
and knowing nothing of the world,
knowing less because it was a world
void of recording every breath of itself,
and so stupidity could be clandestine
until
one decided to move away
and learn
that there were beliefs other than Catholicism,
skin colors other than our own,
different spices to captivate our tongues,
that humanity existed in all forms
that maybe had been cloistered
in similar ways,
in neighborhoods that were rarely ventured out of,

perhaps many also fatherless
with working single mothers
going from job to job to job,
perhaps drinking too much,
perhaps angry too much,
but in cities
the many worlds would somehow converge,
and arguments and pleasantries would be exchanged,
handshakes and smiles
and shoves and grins,
awareness blanketing ignorance,
with sometimes the latter prevailing,
and maybe even a friendship would unfold
and, out of that,
would be discovered
a greater part
of this world,
if not to love
then at least
to respect.

Akin to Thornton Wilder
(6/12/20)

Maybe the upshot
was that things slowed a bit
and gave us a chance
to reside in the moment
as opposed to
watching our lives in reruns,
like Emily in *Our Town*
who pleaded for the memory
of her mother
making breakfast.

"Karen" in Wisconsin
(6/13/20)

A lawyer
from Wisconsin
spat
in the face
of a
17 year-old
black teen
claiming
that she was a cancer survivor
and *"he
wasn't
wearing a mask."*

Mind you,
neither
was
she.

Campaign of Ashes
(6/14/20)

In Tulsa,
where a little over 99 years ago
there were 35 charred blocks
of where blacks had once thrived,
the elephants
plan to trample
and say they've beaten the virus
and created law and order
and brought back jobs
and kept the Mexicans out
and the children wrapped in foil
and will make America
even greater
in November.

Supply and Demand
(6/15/20)

Street tables along
5th Avenue
in Sunset Park
continue to sell rubbing alcohol
and surgical masks
and disposable gloves
from where empanadas
and fried maize
were once featured,
as passersby glance
at the sad eyes
of the unpermitted vendors,
famished
for the past.

The Birds
(6/16/20)

Green leaves
look at me
through my window
with its chirping occupants
oblivious
to illness and disharmony,
or maybe
they know it
as well,
even more,
and just
don't get
the coverage.

Green
(6/17/20)

It has always
hoed
and seeded
the American soil,
working against
the many who've toiled;
it's disregarded
and deprived
and ignored
and bribed
and kept the fences up
and revoked
and let drowned
and croaked,
it's given money
so that money can make money;
oh, the sweet American honey
that has oozed out of the trees and hives
and blindfolded the eyes
of those on the hill,
what to submerge,
who to kill,
as the green river flows
but passes the poor,
it breaks through levees
and destroys even more,
and when the monsoon ends
and the sun returns,
the missiles will remain pointed;
a lesson never learned,
waiting for an enemy
to justify
the green that flows through the country's veins,
for as long as we live
and die.

A Not Quite Haiku
(6/18/20)

---

4 days
before our second phase,
humidity cascades
as caution
fades.

Juneteenth
(6/19/20)

Friday
wafts in the windows,
a day
and history at once,
and one wonders
what such liberation
means now,
what lies ahead
and all that
confederate shovels
look
to inter
and exhume.

A Civil Emergency
(6/20/20)

They've camped out for days
in the mossy rain
to be among the thousands who will gather
in the Tulsa heat,
with masks
and sanitizers
and distancing
optional,
like extra cheese
or a baked potato,
while the only requirement
is red hats
and posters
of the Orange Emperor
posed like Rambo
with black garb,
adorned in ammunition,
despite gatherers
warned by scientists
that the curve
will become as vertical
as a flag pole,
saluted by loyal negligence,
while protesters
are warned
that they
can be killed
before the virus
has a chance
to embrace their lungs;
now a civil emergency
has been declared,

for this has become

the perfect storm.

Father's Day, Part II
(6/21/20)

You were gone
before you were gone,
yet today
I'm to display
photos of us
in happier times,
of which I have
none.

On Sweltering Summer Nights
(6/22/20)

Now that there are bigger
fish to fry
in this city
of protests
and fading illness,
with the dusk
comes
the booms,
pops
and crackles
that rain
like a new war
of the unseen
that recalls
the old lawless nights
of New York City
when one could walk two blocks
and lose an ear
without batting an eye
weeks before
and after
the 4th of July,
and no one knew any more
than they do now
why this was done,
other than sheer boredom
on a sweltering
summer night.

Of Magritte Proportions
(6/23/20)

The older one gets,
the more one sees
floating green apples,
flying baguettes,
ascending bowler hats,
that a pipe is not a pipe
and clouds and blue skies
are faces,
and nothing is everything,
and silence is deafening
and life fades,
as do the days,
on a canvas
by an unseen hand,
and, strangely,
it all
makes
sense.

The Harder They Fall
(6/24/20)

the bronze,
the marble,
the alabaster
are pulled down
and decapitated
and burned
and drowned
and hung
and defaced,
as the earth trembles
like a steady seizure
due to the crashing history
permeating the states,
or is it the flesh
that has been
pulled down
and decapitated
and burned
and drowned
and hung
and defaced,
and we're just now
noticing?

4am, on 45th
(6/25/20)

Silence,
until
the clinks and clangs
of cans and bottles
rummaged,
before the street
awakens
with sand
in its eyes.

Be Still, She Says
(6/26/20)

Across my lap,
you lay
and keep me sane,
closed eyes
peeking
at any movement
that deviates from
a flipped page.

Independence Day
(6/27/20)

The 2:30am
booms and crackles
keep eyes open
in Brooklyn
night
after night
into morning
after morning,
making Independence Day seem
redundant
and redundant.

Still in the Woods
(6/28/20)

The storm's eye
doesn't blink;
it gazes
undeterred,
a wave
fed
and led
by foolishness,
whose gusts
will all the more
excel
when one
expels,
knowing not of
warmth or cold
or young or old;
it is simply
there,
even after these
many months,
unwilling to be escorted away,
like an unwanted guest,
it will stay
until saner heads prevail
on stronger legs
to gouge the unflinching iris
of this
plague.

18 Years
(6/29/20)

I'll make us blueberry pancakes this morning
and we'll sit by your red and yellow roses
with coffee,
limited to where we can venture now,
we may simply stay home
and watch the rain
and be together
and recall 18 years
and I'll thank you for your tolerance,
thank you for being my friend,
thank you for loving me
and for holding my hand
and jumping into this
unpredictable canyon
called matrimony
and continuing to navigate
through the valleys and rolling hills
as the doves imbibe
from the makeshift troth
on our fire escape
and many dreams wait to be obtained,
ones which will one day arrive,
perhaps without fanfare,
but they'll be there, soon –
and I'll be with you,
still holding your hand.

104 Days of the Pandemic, or Happy Birthday to Me
(6/30/20)

This 104th day
is also my 50th year,
and I suppose it behooves me
to compose
this living eulogy,
this ode to something;
so strange, this life,
what one comes from,
what fades with the tide,
making sense of the nonsense,
lemonade from lemons;
the years leading up to this day
seem like an oiled ladder I've climbed
that I look up
and see the rungs
beyond the powdered sugar clouds;
so much more to go,
the steps staring down at me,
daring me to continue,
and I want to,
despite the dents in
my half-century armor
and the last 104 days of a storm
that will continue
beyond this poem;
indeed, I've embraced the sudden stillness,
and would lie if I said
I didn't mind the deceleration of the world,
if only it weren't
for *this*,
but tragedy knows no speed
nor constraint,
we just never think it'll be
today,
yet sometimes it is,

and then the levees break,
though we imagine we'll rise above it,
and often do,
and I think today
how I wish I knew
what I now know
at 40,
at 30,
and yet reflection is only a memory in stone
that all the chiseling cannot shape into
something else,
but if I plan to continue,
not in the future,
but now,
only now,
and savor these breaths for their sweetness,
love what needs to be loved,
don't look up or down
or at the demons in the periphery
or the mirror that shows no proof,
and, instead,
look at an old oak tree
that may teach me more
than anything,
…then these 50 years
will not have been
for naught.

Daniel Damiano is an Award-winning Playwright, Screenwriter, Poet, Actor and Novelist based in Brooklyn, NY. His plays have been performed throughout many areas of the U.S., as well as London, England and Sydney & Melbourne, Australia. His acclaimed play *DAY OF THE DOG* premiered with St. Louis Actors' Studio in 2013 and subsequently transferred to 59E59 in NYC in 2014. It was a 2013 St. Louis Critics Choice Best Play Nominee and was published by Broadway Play Publishing in 2018. Other more recent productions of his work include *HARMONY PARK* ("4 Stars" - Detroit Free Press, with Detroit Repertory Theatre), *THE LEPERS* (Ensemble Studio Theatre, NYC) and his acclaimed solo play *AMERICAN TRANQUILITY* (which has been lauded in both NYC and Washington DC). His new play *THE WILD BOAR* was a 2019 Finalist for both the Woodward/Newman Award and the Janet & Bruce Bunch Award. He was a 2013 Nominee for the Pushcart Poetry Prize and a Finalist for the 2012 Arts & Letters Prize for Drama. His debut novel, *THE WOMAN IN THE SUN HAT* was published in March 2021 through fandango 4 Art House. His short story, *"The Gift of What For"* was published in Palm Circle Press' Short Story Anthology in May 2021. His poetry has thus far been published in Crooked Teeth Literary Magazine, Newtown Literary Journal, New Voices Anthology, Cloudbank and HotMetal Press.

www.ingramcontent.com/pod-product-compliance
Lightning Source LLC
Chambersburg PA
CBHW051450290426
44109CB00016B/1701